To be healthy, you must eat enough food and the right kinds of food.

Good eating gives you plenty of energy and helps you to keep fit and to grow.

Each day, you should have many different kinds of food.

Milk helps you to have strong bones and teeth and gives you lots of energy for playing games and working.

There are several kinds of milk. Each bottle has a coloured cap to show what kind of milk it is.

Fruit and custard

Milkshake

Banana

Scotch pancakes

Silver top has all the cream left in. Blue and silver check-topped milk has the cream skimmed away.

As well as drinking it plain, you can have milk in custard, pancakes, rice pudding and other cooked foods. There are lots of exciting flavours to try in milkshakes, too!

Milk

Rice pudding

These are some of the foods that are made from milk.

Cream is collected by skimming off the top of the milk. Butter is made by spinning the cream round and round in a churn.

Cheese and yogurt are more solid forms of milk.

Dairy cow

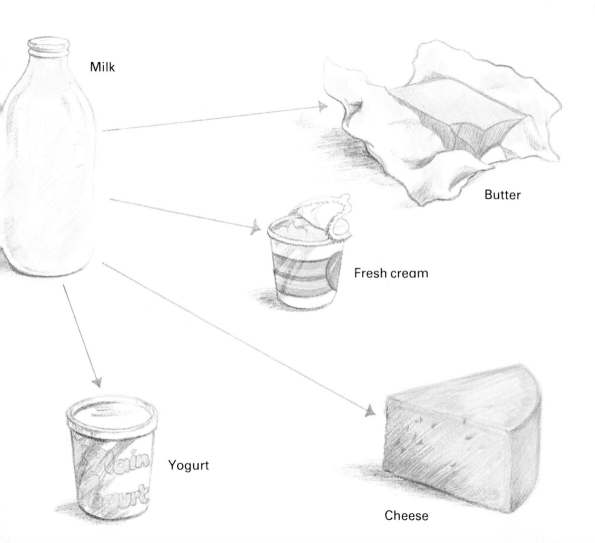

Milk

Butter

Fresh cream

Yogurt

Cheese

Yogurt makes a good snack because it has all the goodness of milk in it.

You can use yogurt as a topping for puddings – it's very good on fresh fruit. Try making your own snack by putting chopped fresh fruit into a dish of yogurt.

Apple

Raspberries

Banana

Strawberries

Pear

Plain yogurt

Fruit yogurt

Orange

Plums

Carton of yogurt

There are different kinds of cheese named after the places where they were first made. Cheddar cheese is famous all over the world.

Cheese is good to eat by itself in chunks, or in sandwiches. Cooked meals, like cauliflower cheese and macaroni cheese, are very tasty, too.

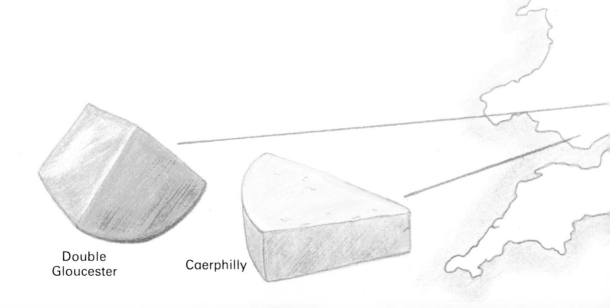

Double
Gloucester

Caerphilly

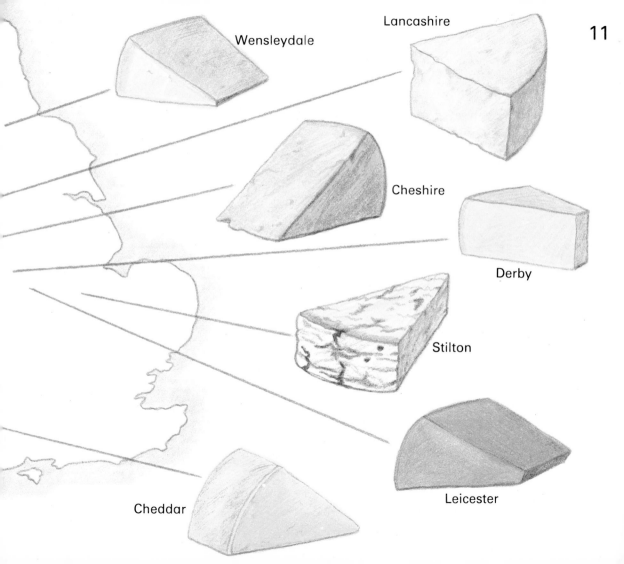

Wensleydale

Lancashire

11

Cheshire

Derby

Stilton

Cheddar

Leicester

There is another group of foods and you should try to eat some of these each day. These are bread, breakfast cereals, rice, and pasta (spaghetti and macaroni). Choose the brown kinds if you can.

Brown rice with peppers

Brown spaghetti with mushrooms

These foods give you lots of energy and help you to grow. They also have fibre in them to help you to digest your food.

Breakfast cereal

Brown bread

Salad sandwich

You should eat plenty of vegetables every day.
They contain fibre and important vitamins to
help you grow.

There are hundreds of kinds of vegetables –
carrots, beans, cabbage, peas, potatoes, lettuce,
cucumber, celery and watercress are just a
few!

How many others have you tried?

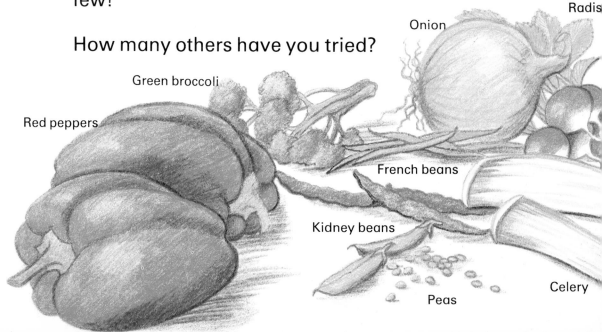

Radis

Onion

Green broccoli

Red peppers

French beans

Kidney beans

Celery

Peas

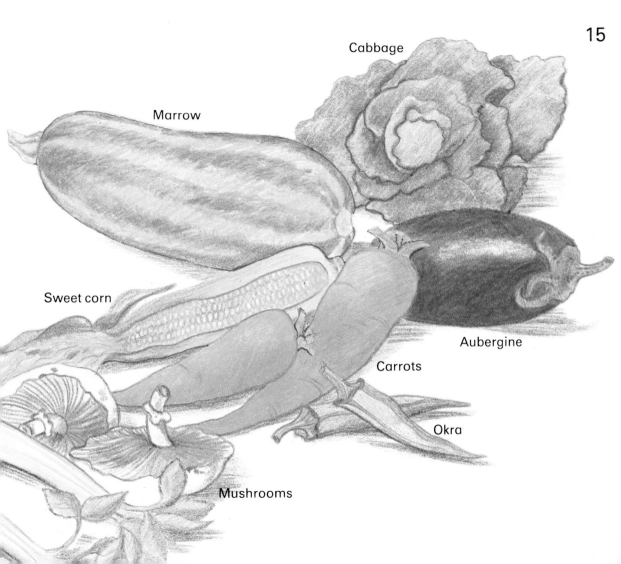

Cabbage

Marrow

Sweet corn

Aubergine

Carrots

Okra

Mushrooms

Potatoes can be boiled, mashed or baked in their jackets. They can also be roasted or made into chips, but you should try not to eat fried food too often.

Vegetable soup

Meat, mashed potatoes, carrots and Brussels sprouts

Baked beans on toast

Uncooked vegetables are good to eat. Raw carrots make a quick snack, and salads with a main meal are always tasty.

Mixed salad

Jacket potatoes with cheese

Fruit is delicious. It helps to give you a clear, healthy skin, shiny hair and bright eyes.

There are many sorts of fruit to choose from and everyone should try to eat two kinds each day.

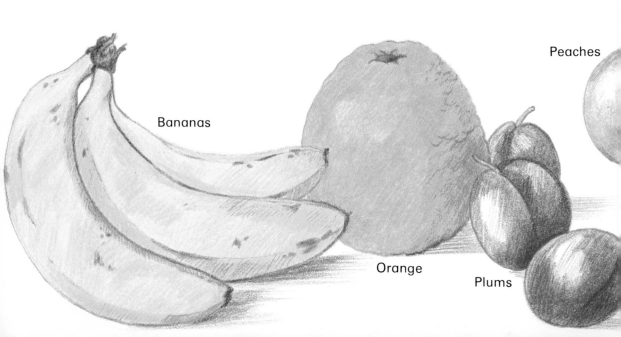

Peaches

Bananas

Orange

Plums

19

Pineapple

Pear

Apple

Melon

Grapes

Raspberries

Strawberries

There are some foods which are very good for building your body. These are fish, meat, and eggs. Fish is especially good for you.

There are different ways of cooking these – they can be boiled, steamed, grilled, baked or fried.

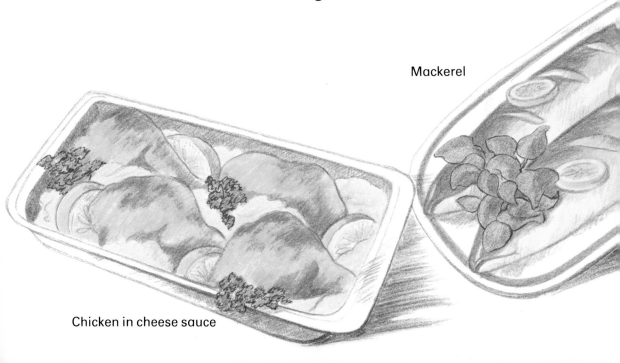

Mackerel

Chicken in cheese sauce

Some people prefer not to eat meat and fish. They are called vegetarians because they eat vegetables such as lentils, peas and different kinds of beans. They also eat cheese and other foods made from milk.

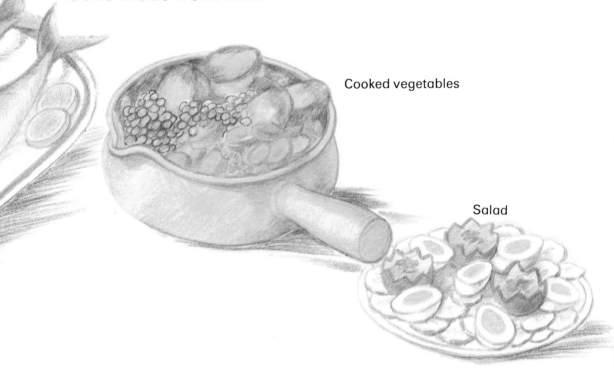

Cooked vegetables

Salad

If you feel hungry between meals and need
something to fill you up try one of these:
A glass of milk
A sandwich
A small piece of cheese
A piece of fruit
A pot of yogurt

A few more tips:
Try to eat a good breakfast each day.
Don't have too many fizzy drinks.
Don't miss meals.
Don't nibble too many biscuits, cakes,
crisps or sweets.
Get plenty of sleep and fresh air.

Good health!